# Table of Contents

Rourke
Educational Media

A Division of
Carson
Dellosa
Education

rourkeeducationalmedia.com

# Can you find these words?

explore

hair

puppies

swats

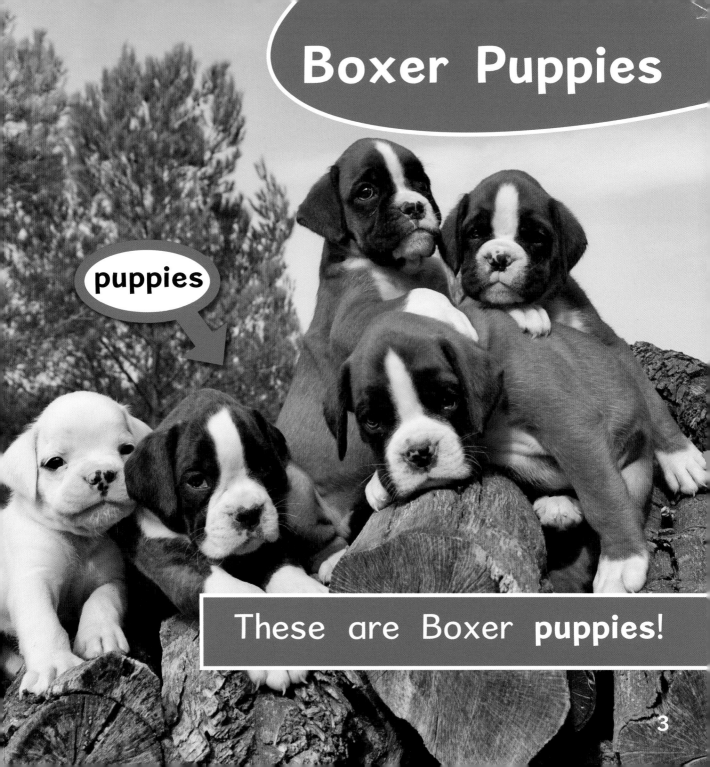

What do Boxer puppies look like?

4

Their faces have a square shape.

What do Boxer puppies act like?

They are curious.
They like to **explore**.

explore

swats

They want to play.

This puppy **swats** at a friend.

11

They need people.

They are part of the family.

# Did you find these words?

They like to **explore**.

They have short **hair**.

These are Boxer **puppies**!

This puppy **swats** at a friend.

# Photo Glossary

 **explore** (ik-SPLOR): To travel and look around to find things.

 **hair** (hair): Thin strands that grow from the body.

 **puppies** (PUHP-eez): Dogs that are young and not fully grown.

 **swats** (swahts): Hits with a quick blow.

# Index

# About the Author

Hailey Scragg is a writer from Ohio. She loves all puppies, especially her puppy, Abe! She likes taking him on long walks in the park.

www.rourkeeducationalmedia.com

PHOTO CREDITS: cover: ©2windspa, ©manley099 (bone); back cover: ©zhobla91 (inset), ©Naddiya (pattern); pages 2, 3, 8-9, 14, 15: ©cynoclub; pages 4-5: ©JLSnader; pages 2, 6-7, 14, 15: ©Astrid Schur; pages 2, 10-11, 14, 15: ©Betty4240; pages 12-13: ©lewkmiller

Edited by: Kim Thompson
Cover and interior design by: Janine Fisher

**Library of Congress PCN Data**
Boxer Puppies / Hailey Scragg
(Top Puppies)
ISBN 978-1-73162-873-2 (hard cover)(alk. paper)
ISBN 978-1-73162-872-5 (soft cover)
ISBN 978-1-73162-874-9 (e-Book)
ISBN 978-1-73163-345-3 (ePub)
Library of Congress Control Number: 2019944973

Printed in the United States of America,
North Mankato, Minnesota